Contents

A
Floristry
of
Palpitations

George Stanworth
has been writing
poetry since his
teens, but he
started developing
it further when he
studied English
Literature at
University. This is
George's third

collection of poetry, following on from
Crazy Old World and *Your Sax Is On Fire*.
George has previously performed at the
Edinburgh Fringe, and is a regular
performer in pubs around London and the
Home Counties. George has also been a
six-times semi-finalist in the Lyrics Only
section of the 'UK Songwriting Contest';
and has been published in numerous
anthologies, including *The Haiku Journal*
and *Sarasvati* magazine.

www.georgestanworth.com

Other titles from deserthearts.com:

Flowers

I picked Van Gogh's Sunflowers
and Peploe's Tulips
then arranged them like the
perfect wedding day.

I tied the bouquet together
with kisses from eternity,
and wrapped them in moonlight
from your favourite landscape.

I presented them to you
like a Jane Austen hero,
as your eyes lit up
my universe.

I waited like the stars await their fate.

First Date

There's fragrance in your laughter.
Your Bluebell eyes are fresh
and lively, lifting my smile
above your soul.
My heart skips like a child
untainted by life, as your
Iris dress sways in the May breeze.
Your Primrose mind enchants me
as the Tulip words
bloom off your tongue.
Is it a dare or a bet?
Howcome you picked me,
some hedgebank Toadflax,
shunned throughout my life.

Over-Reaction

It wasn't like the ice-caps had melted
or the rainbows in meadows had wilted.
      I never bought the bread.

It wasn't like the Nile had turned to dust
or the sun was controlled by militants.
      I'd only made a list.

It wasn't like McDonald's had bought the
naming rights for Mother Nature.
      I didn't fold the clothes.

It wasn't like all bird song disappeared
or the honey bees were all destroyed.
      I'd yelled that Gerrard scored.

It wasn't like the clouds were stalking us
or oxygen had affairs with syphilis.
      You asked for fries not mash.

It wasn't like the earth was voted out
of a contest where we must all bid adieu.
      I just said I love you.

Frost At Twilight

Winter scenery
weaved
between your
pauses.

Icicles hung
from your
intervals
as frostbite
consonants
fragmented.

Arctic air
orchestrated
speech,
cracking
frozen syllables.

Surgical silence
snapped
as reality
threw
snowballs
through my gangrene
heart.

Too Many Songs

Every time I'm clubbing.
or playing on my Wii,
I just think of music
written just for me.

Every time I meditate.
Every time there's hope.
I just think of lyrics
that tell me how to cope.

There's too many songs
that remind me of you.
Too many songs
that are painfully true.

There's too many songs
in the world these days.
Too many songs
that I'd like to erase.

Sometimes when I'm running,
or swigging all my wine.
I think of all our history
when everything was fine.

Sometimes I feel sunshine,
and everlasting fame.
Then someone hums a tune too close
that makes me sad again.

There's too many songs
that remind me of you.
Too many songs
that are painfully true.

There's too many songs
in the world these days.
Too many songs
that I'd like to erase.

Situation Vacant

WE NOW HAVE A VACANCY FOR A NEW
COMMUTER.

ESSENTIAL SKILLS & EXPERIENCE:

- 5 years pushing experience.
- 5 years exaggerated sighing experience.
- The ability to stand on the left hand side of the escalator rather than walking down it.
- Experience of shouting 'No! You're a twat!'
- Growling when another commuter requests for you to move your bag off the seat next to you, even though it is a packed train with half the passengers standing on each other's heads, and having their noses up each other's arses.
- The ability to ignore any other commuter who asks you for money.

DESIRABLE SKILLS & EXPERIENCE:

- The ability to use an iPod, iPad, or iPanty.
- An ability to raise your blood pressure beyond an acceptable level when other commuters attempt to board the tube before you get off.
- An ability to turn an accidental trip into something you intended to do.
- Pretending to be asleep when the ticket inspector arrives in a mistaken belief he will walk past you, because you can't be arsed to look for your ticket.
- Maintaining a dignified silence when someone has let one off.
- Ignoring others even when they start a conversation with you.
- Shutting off from everyone else by listening to music.
- Texting experience would go in your favour but is not essential.
- The ability to use a train toilet correctly would also go in your favour, but again, not essential.

I Saw Your CV Earlier

I saw your CV earlier –
The best one on the site,
I have an opportunity,
I think that you will like.

It's situated locally
(well 50 miles away)
and fits your profile perfectly
(except on role and pay).

But those are just some minor points,
I'm sure that you agree
the most important things these days
are perks for you and me.

I can't disclose the ones I get
but yours will make you drool,
for once a month you get to leave
five minutes early, 'Cool!'

Their bonus scheme is excellent.
I think they have the edge
It's never failed to pay out once
(although it's fruit and veg).

They also give you so much more,
like lunchbreaks and some leave.
This is the best role that I have.
Oh please, you must believe.

Please say you'll go for interview.
Please tell me your position.
I know you need it, need it more
than my need for commission!

First Day Questions

On my first day at work I wondered if David Moyes also had an IT induction at Manchester United. Did David Cameron go livid because Gordon Brown had forgotten to leave him handover documentation? Was Noel Edmonds' banker phone set up for him, or did he have to speak to 4 different people to get it arranged? Did Danny Dyer have to make the cast of EastEnders a cup of tea in order to fit in? Was Fireman Sam told where all the Fire Exits were, or did his manager just assume he would know? Did Bob the Builder get appropriate health and safety training? Did any of these people ever contemplate resigning after 45 minutes?

The Presentation

A floristry of palpitations blossom
tiredly. Laundered thoughts squat on latte
stained notes, infecting the puddle scent mind.
Stumbling syllables velcro tongue caught,
mock sentences sterile and taught. Indexed
movements of rehearsals commence, tainting
toad infested palms. Curbed eyes and puppet
earthquake digits present your blissful bleached life .

Commuting By Train's Much Better Than War

Staring at screens stating 'Cancelled/Delayed',
hearing apologies 'Blue Peter' made.
Stranded on platforms in missile like rain,
whilst waiting for lights to turn green once again.
>Commuting by train's a little like pain.

Six per cent rises, and still not on time,
train comes then stops due to trespassers crime.
Someone swigs Stella and belches so vile
that words are exchanged like on Jeremy Kyle.
>Commuting by train's a little like piles.

My head in an armpit, arm stuck in seat,
my daily commute is truly a treat.
I come to my stop, but can't reach the door.
I moan, but a man with one arm starts to roar:-
>Commuting by train's much better than war.
>Commuting by train's much better than war.

Party Political Games

David Cameron and Nick Clegg
played Mario Kart.
The PM was Bowser. His No.2 – Princess Peach.

John Major sulked.
He wanted to play Daley Thompson's Decathlon.

Cameron and Clegg just laughed
and mocked him for being way behind the times.

Barack Obama told them to simmer down
as it was time for bed.

Clegg sucked his thumb
and Cameron pondered what benefits to cut next.

A Party Popper Political Broadcast

Hic! Hic! Hooray!
Hic!
Our manifesto is this.
more fizz,
get pissed,
and randomly shout
'Hooray!'

Squeeze the day
and mix it with a
'Whey-Hey-Hey!'
Laugh, have fun, and let the moonlight rhyme.
Party like it's nineteen ninety, nineteen, ninety wine.

Hic!
Pick us.
We're lush,
and can't be hushed,

We're truthful, and have never lied.
Authentic, not a bit contrived.

I sometimes dream about Todd Carty –
Vote for us, the 'POPPER PARTY!'

The Perils Of Intergalactic Integration

Galloping galaxies spreading lies too,
brain cleanse their voters
to retain deposits;
appearing like igloos in Rio.

They make up new words
to woo their fanactics,
then promise no harm to 'anti-them' planets,
and pledge what they cannot afford.

Minds photocopy and duplicate past,
disguising through waffle the actual cost,
whilst changing the subject to moon bumping sleaze.

Like marathon day where numerous enter
only the favourites will ever succeed.
Political baggers have odds long as death,
but none of this matters, and seems to deter
ridiculous parties like 'Martians Love Craters'
participating as certain time-wasters.

Electorate conned from planet to space,
convinced as galaxies integrate,
there's more selection for each voice.
A Billion parties but still no choice!

Out Of Touch

They thought the sun was a wheel
and tried to clamp it.
Half of it escaped unharmed.

Meals on wheels were not so lucky.
Motionless for hours –
many people starved that day.

Wagon Wheels were found at pounds,
melting in the heat –
waiting for liberation.

The Wheel of Fortune
could not be filmed and turned away
disappointed contestants.

National Wheel Clamping Day
was not well received,
so another one's been arranged!

Manhole Cover

'No more taxes that's a pledge.
No more wars to spark outrage.
No more   . Trust my word.
No   afford.
No more   . That's guaranteed.'
No more promises believed.

Resignation

All the oak trees want to touch the sky, the puddles to be lakes;
when their dreams fail to materialise, they sulk, and then they
    break.
The clouds want to be higher, and fields as tall as hills
Their aims hurt Mother Nature, so of course that's why she's ill.

So don't let me know the password anymore for fragile earth
I'll return my badge then exit to a planet with self-worth.
I won't come back for a meeting so I sign in as a guest.
I've seen how earth promotes itself and I'm really not impressed.

All the deserts seem to need more sand to satisfy its greed
and the weather thinks of image more than helping those in
    need.
All the thistles are not comfortable with how they look each day
and seagulls always strive to sound and sing the songbird way.

So don't let me know the password anymore for fragile earth
I'll return my badge then exit to a planet with self-worth.
I won't come back for a meeting so I sign in as a guest.
I've seen how earth promotes itself and I'm really not impressed.

I fear the superficial seas
and every egotistic breeze.
I hate the way the gloomy sky
is marketed as one big lie . . .

So don't let me know the password anymore for fragile earth
I'll return my badge then exit to a planet with self-worth.
I won't come back for a meeting so I sign in as a guest.
I've seen how earth promotes itself and I'm really not impressed.
I've seen how earth promotes itself and I'm really not impressed.

Concrete Characters

They cloned imagination
and sold it for a profit.
They hyped enthusiasm
until we all went off it.

They placed originality
under microscopes
and came up with a formula
that conformists understood.

They ridiculed each sunrise mind,
each solstice look,
each best day thought,
each tuneful hook.

Like each Gorgon turned to stone,
concrete characters have grown;

influencing how we think
until free thoughts are all extinct

They cloned imagination
and sold it for a profit.
They hyped enthusiasm
until we all forgot it.

They placed originality
under microscopes
and came up with a formula
that conformists understood.

They marketed our laughter,
but this was not enough.
They printed all affection
and photocopied love.

Like each Gorgon turned to stone,
concrete characters have grown;

Like each Gorgon turned to stone,
concrete characters have grown;

More and more on the attack
My spirit though remains intact!

There's Another Person Leaving

There's another person leaving.
The firm's as cool as thieving.
So I know what I'm receiving –
      Another card to sign.

He only started yesterday.
I never met him anyway.
So what the hell am I to say?
      'You're the fastest to resign!'

The comments range from 'It's a Shame'
to 'All the best' and 'Call again!'
But no one seems to know your name.
      'Dude. Better luck next time.'

And then an envelope appears
But none of our cash disappears,
as there are disapproving jeers.
      And now I think, you swine!

He only started yesterday.
We never met him anyway.
So none of us are gonna pay.
      Our messages aren't kind.

Instead we buy some lunchtime wine
and have a bloody jolly time.
We slag him off. It's not a crime!
          We don't care if he minds.

There's another person leaving.
We're less likeable than grieving
or Percy Whitmore's breathing.
          We found out he was blind!

Training Courses Available

☛ **Accelerated Procrastination**	*Info:* Course currently on hold.
☛ **Managing Change (the Sir Alex Ferguson Way)**	*Duration:* 1 day *(It may slightly overrun depending on Sir Alex's watch).*
☛ **Essential Bullshitting**	*Cost:* £10 – Yeah, really!
☛ **Shifting Blame Effectively**	*Cost:* £15,000 *(Contact Maureen if you have any concerns about the cost as I have only just started).*
☛ **How to Be More Efficient at Work**	*Duration:* Every other hour for 100 weeks.
☛ **Motivate Yourself by De-Motivating Your Staff**	*Info:* Please bring along the weakest member of your team.
☛ **Corporate Ladder-Climbing for Those Overlooked**	*Duration:* 50 years.
☛ **Treating Others with Dignity and Respect**	*Info:* Please note that our training facilities have no toilets, but there will be a toilet in the corner if you need to relieve yourself.
☛ **Certificate in Acting You Have Drunk Less than You Really Have at Lunchtime**	*Info:* Please bring your own alcohol.
☛ **Obtaining Information about Projects You Should Be Involved In**	*Info:* Currently unavailable.

Blameless

Yes, I don't do the job that you ask,
and flunk every bog-standard task.
Yes, I tell you I won't go and see,
important clients, but don't blame me –
      It's your fault for employing me.

Yes, I know that I'm always in late,
and sometimes bring yesterday's date.
Yes, I know that I won't go and see
a counsellor, but don't blame me –
      It's your fault for employing me.

Yes, I know that I won't see HR
because their office is not in a bar,
Yes, I know that you want to sack me
but here's betting the appeal board agree
      It was your fault for employing me!

The Appraisal

Your printer cartridge face was low on ink.
Woodwork Wednesday's resurfaced, pacing your
breath like a cross-country runner chased by
Frankenstein's monster. Swimming gala's drowned
your future. Binary Normans charged through
your spleen, mashing the past into now. The
stench of lumpy custard seeped out as you
waited. Last rites were performed by tortured
artists bullied by convention. Dali
walked in. Your CPU was far too high.

You Told Me That You Could Not Wait

You told me that you could not wait
until we met up for our date.
You'd have your wicked way 'til late.
You text my number by mistake!

E-Fail

You sent me
flowers as an
attachment
to my email
account.

It wasn't
quite the
romantic
gesture
I was
looking for.

I replied
with a
JPEG of a
dump.

I never
received
a postmaster
failure
email
back
so you must have got the message.

Hate Date

"If you were some transport – what would it be?
Would it be in the air, on the ground, or on sea?"
"I'd be a milk float – is that worth a tick?"
Shocked by response she was physically sick!

I Know How To Fail - I've Failed Before

I'm in debt, and been a devil,
got an 'N' grade at A-Level.
Walked out on my driving lessons,
got no ticks in dating sessions.

There's not much that I know for sure,
but I know how to fail – I've failed before.
So if you read my rhyme no more,
then I won't be sad. I've failed before.

My poems get rejected fast,
I can't perform a simple task,
like putting up a shelf or frame –
achievements are tough to obtain.

There's not much that I know for sure,
but I know how to fail – I've failed before.
So if you read my rhyme no more,
then I won't be sad. I've failed before.

Life is pants
for those like me
who lose out more
than they succeed.
We try our best
to be supreme
but have the genes
of Mr Bean

There's not much that I know for sure,
but I know how to fail – I've failed before.
So if you read my rhyme no more,
I won't be sad. I've failed before!

One Letter Makes
A Difference

One letter makes a difference to a word as we all know.
I would never trust an Editor who mixed up 'Sew' with 'Sow'.
A 'Lollipup' would be obscene, a pack of 'Sweats' disgusting.
A lunchtime 'Cornish Nasty' – well that's not one I'm trusting!

One letter changes meanings of a word as we all know.
I would never want a ribbon tied in bogs instead of bows.
I would never want a heliday, or have a trap abroad,
or my team to buy a striker who snored but never scored

One letter makes a difference to a word as we all know.
Who would want some falling snot instead of falling snow?
Who would drink some 'Hater', or have some 'Lemonape'?
Who buy a milkshame or drink some strawberry snake?

One letter changes meanings of a word as we all know.
Athletes would be so confused with 'Ready, Steady, No!'
'Farts' would be a smelly sport and 'Footwall' would be bold.
But everyone would celebrate if golf turned into gold!

You Owned
That Lawn

You dug your lawn
so it resembled the letter 'X'.
You hoped to attract Simon Cowell.

Aliens the size of
two Peter Crouches
appeared instead.

They thought
they had found
the buried treasure.

Louis Walsh reminded you
that you owned that lawn –

You did – but now the aliens do.

Old Ladies Don't Tolerate That

I went to bingo and shouted out 'Flat',
after only one number. Flo called me a 'Tw%t'!

"What Time Is Jake Bugg's gig?"

I looked on the net for a wig,
but ended up buying a pig.

Delia's Advice Just Cannot Be Beat

How to eat some sweets?
Put one in your mouth – repeat.

Professor Green Bin Goes Out This Week

"That budgie's got a snout-like beak."
"It's a piglet, not a budgie – freak!"

I Love You More Than Final Score

I love you more than Smirnoff Ice,
Kronenbourg, and Egg Fried Rice.

I love you more than apps and games,
cars and trucks, and cranes and trains.
I love you more than childish jokes
and pool games with some random blokes.

I love you more than custard creams,
ham and chips with Heinz Baked Beans.

I love you more than Ayia Napa,
porn and every gangster rapper.

I love you greatly that's for sure,
but not when watching 24.

I'll always love Jack Bauer more!

Naivety

Don't hurt me like you do.
I'm only human, but
at time like these,
I have to think –
are you?

Kidnapped By A Public House

A Public House abducted me
and wouldn't let me go.
It forced me to down twenty pints
then 5 shots in a row.

It tortured me with Scampi Fries
then dragged me to play pool.
It tied me down onto the stage,
and made me act the fool.

It said that I must give my thoughts
on playing 4-3-3,
and threatened me with cards and darts
if I did not agree.

It spun me round the room so fast
and made me feel like trash.
It stripped me to my boxer shorts
then took away my cash.

I never thought I would escape,
but then it let me free.
There were a dozen hostages
released along with me.

I know it seems a bit far fetched,
like meeting Captain Kirk,
but really that's the reason why
I'm always late for work!

I Can't Believe It's Not Bitter

'Kerrygold' and 'Anchor'
were poured to my surprise,
and all because I sometimes
mix my U's up with my I's.

Delete As Appropriate

Dress down Friday
did not mean coming in to
work without your trousers.

You were sacked on the spot
but won the tribunal on penalties.

You worked elsewhere,
and on day one
you wore two pairs of trousers
(just incase.)

You were sacked on the spot.

Your new job was
as a stripper/ in a nudist colony (delete as appropriate. I don't
really care. Nobody ever reads my stuff anyway!)

Changing Your Career Must Always Be Thought Through

Changing your career must always be thought through,
for what you've done already affects what you can do.
Who would trust a minister who used to sell old cars.
Who'd prefer a teacher who once stripped in the bars.

Changing your career is not as easy as it sounds,
as there's some you should avoid if you used to be a clown.
It may not be acceptable to be an undertaker,
High Court judge, a lawyer, or a city money maker.

Changing your career must always be thought through ,
for what you've done already affects what you next do.
Who would want a fitness coach who was a showbiz waster
Who would want a Chauffeur who was a banger racer.

Changing your career is not as easy as it sounds.
A former darts world champ should not advise on losing pounds.
Who would want librarians who used to be town-criers.
Who would want a stunt-man who used to put out fires.

Changing your career is not always for the best.
It may not bring you happiness, or guarantee success.
Giving up a stable job to be a TV star,
For 99% of us won't take us very far.

Changing your career must always be thought through ,
for what you've done already affects what you next do.

The Corporate Poet

Employee number 312 –
Your pension scheme's eroding.
Your salary's unpaid this week,
an error in the coding.

Employee number 312 –
Your bonuses are halving.
There's plenty to be grateful for.
Your children are not starving.

Employee number 312 –
Your gossip's overflowing.
We're sacking you – and as you leave,
these lines should keep you going.

Your Office Was Smaller Than Others

Your office was smaller than others.
Your ego was somewhat destroyed.
You would have been quitting that evening
If you hadn't just gone self-employed.

Game Shows And How They Apply In The Workplace

SORRY I HAVEN'T A CLUE:
IT Help Desk.

THE MILLION POUND DROP :
Bankers who lose their bonuses.

15 To 1:
The number of people in the department 12 months ago compared with today.

COUNTDOWN:
Only 6 hours and 57 minutes until home time!

HAVE I GOT NEWS FOR YOU:
The office gossip is back.

WIPEOUT:
The company pension has completely disappeared.

THE CHASE:
Trying to catch up with those actually responsible for the project.

WOULD I LIE TO YOU?:
A recruitment agent over-selling a role.

POINTLESS:
Office Suggestion Boxes.

ODD ONE OUT:
The employee who does not go to the pub after work.

Jim Bowen's Arrow

He entered the pub
with raffle tickets
for another Speedboat
he had available.

Customers were amazed
that after hosting 'Bullseye'
for so long, he took
an Archer's approach
to playing darts.

Has It Been A Year Since We Last Had Sex?

Paul Daniels said 'seven of spades' in his text.
I woke from my coma a little perplexed.

Voices Fell Out Of The Tannoy

"Ship ahoy, ship ahoy, ship ahoy"
Pirates in Millets meditated.

Have You Done The Washing Up Yet?

It was only a quick on-line bet
with your card – now you're thousands in debt.

A Dartboard Was
Your Final Wish

You heard a 'No' but took a risk.
Throwing darts towards the fish.

Have You Heard The News?

Reading papers, weaving across the pavement
is what we British excel in,
and should be on TV for entertainment.
Reading papers, weaving across the pavement
whilst not colliding is an amazement.
If only this was sport we'd win.
Reading papers, weaving across the pavement
is what we British excel in.

First
Performance

I do not choose which memories to retrieve, and when.
Someone I must have offended years ago seems to pick them for
   me.
They restore all the dread and fear from the folders I once
   deleted.

If I tried to sell my insecurities on eBay, they would purchase
   them, and use social media in order to humiliate me
   further.

I don't want to go through with this evening – but if I don't, my
   memory will never let me forget it.

I'm A Performer

I'm a performer.
I love to perform,
when sitting on the toilet,
or stifling a yawn.

I'm a performer.
I love to perform,
when going for confession,
or creeping in at dawn.

I'm a performer.
I love to perform,
when opening a yoghurt,
or when I mow the lawn.

I'm a performer.
I loved to perform,
around my Uncle's death bed
to those that went to mourn.

I'm a performer.
I love to perform,
and ham it up and flounce around
when walking in a storm.

I'm a performer.
I love to perform.
I acted in my Mother's womb,
then more since I was born.

I'm a performer.
I love to perform.
Perhaps that's why I'm single,
and my heart is always torn!

The Envy Of Tom Jones

They threw their handbags at me,
some 'Lockets' and some 'Halls',
a 1980s mobile –
which hit me in the . . . groin!

They chucked at me tomatoes,
unopened in their cans,
and Simon Cowell's comments
(which proved I had few fans).

They lobbed at me their cushions,
plus anger from this morning,
but never any knickers
when I'm doing my performing!

The After-Thought

There once was a farmer from Leeds *(I say Leeds but it may have been Rhyl)*

who liked eating nettles and weeds. *(I say weeds but it may have been dill)*

One day he said 'Yuck. *(In a Yorkshire/North Wales kind of way)*

They taste like pig muck.' *(That's a shit thing to say)*
But he soon became accustomed to *(The ending needs*
its taste. *working on still!)*

The Worst Tutor Ever

There once was a poet called Lee
who said that he always wrote three
lines in his limericks.

I Came
Last

A competition
writing Rondeaus. I came last.
I wrote a Haiku.

The Poem Rejected By Carol Ann Duffy

Murderer!

              You randomly shouted across the bar.

Murderer!

              It was a lucky guess.

You gained a grand and witness protection due to your success.

John Hegley's Not
A Weatherman
(An Apology To The Tribe Of Toffs)

John Hegley's not a weatherman,
a weatherman,
a weatherman.
John Hegley's not a weatherman,
and nor is Michael Rosen . . .

and nor is Roger McGough

and nor is I a n . . . McMillan,

and nor was Wesley Willis.

A Poem A Day Keeps The Public Away

I've written a poem that's better than great.
It's better than any from Larkin or Blake.
I'm sure if you heard it you'd shout out 'Oh Wow!'
And have an orgasm like Meg Ryan now!

I've written a poem that's brilliant I swear.
Carol Ann Duffy just does not compare.
So please stay and listen. Give it a try.
Don't roll your eyeballs and give a big sigh.

I've worked at my craft, and taken my time.
I've also got sonnets, and verses that rhyme
I should be rewarded, gain lots of respect.
So Officer! Officer! Don't go just yet.

And there goes another who won't hear my woes
while I'm working at Primark just selling these clothes.
But at least when it's busy I know what to say,
as a poem a day keeps the public away!

Oblivious

Lord Botox
peeing on
prime time TV.

      The forests need a makeover.

              Vodkas and Stella
              at lunchtime and tea.

      The hills need polishing.

      The sea needs a wash.

Image, a popstar,
Big Brother, a WAG.

      The sky needs repainting.

      The sun has a temperature.

      The landscapes need their nappies changing.

              Let's have a bet –
              Who'll have the first shag?

Sweepstakes and laughter
at who knows the least.

      The seasons need their chakras aligning.

      Natural disasters line up in a queue.

              Vacuous zombies
              puke on the feast.

      Oxygen will fail its M.O.T.

Doubt

Frostbite sky shatters.
Hyperthermia
Claims deserts as
its victim.

'You bastard. You swine.'
bellows memories.
Holiday brochures
Resemble your breath.

Animals dressed
as snow
bounce like
carbon.

I . . .

The instigator
pauses;
but not
from guilt.

The Drought

Cramping clouds wrapped in concrete foam
slow like marathon flops hitting
the wall. Excitement weeps, sitting
      on hilltop throne.

Oaks shelter Ewes, like your repressed
thoughts protected. Fences distressed
fight invisible foes, as closed
      gates moan.

Field hairs droop as pressure builds; sounds
of absence thunders in my mind.
Hedges dampened needed more, and
      rainbow's leave me alone.

The Final Draft

Always seeking synthetic success, for
reasons no psychiatrist is unsure
of. Like Andromeda's black hole, the core
is unstable, and breathes in media whores'
influences and agendas. Your IQ
is beyond atomic numbers, but you
are consumed like an ale in Bavaria.
Past Plutonium thoughts grow scarier,
whilst lost dreams entwine with absent lovers.
Sleeping with ambition is never a droll
one night stand. It clings on, absorbs the soul;
forsaking all others.

Helium Egos

Some think they're superior
because of their exterior,
and act as if they own fresh air
by strutting, posing, flicking hair.

Some make out its intellect
which puts them in the upper set,
and mock those who become confused
through clever choice of words they use.

There are Helium egos around
but most fall back down to the ground.
So when Helium egos go pop
does anyone care where they drop?

Some believe they're best of all
because of all the wealth they maul,
and love to boast at what they mean
by showing off in Limousines.

Some believe it's their career
which puts them in the stratosphere,
and boast of all their contracts won
despite the global damage done.

There are Helium egos around
but most fall back down to the ground.
So when Helium egos go pop
does anyone care where they drop?

It's A Bugger, Life

It's a bugger, life.
It plays catch with those
feelings I'd rather hide,
discard, and refuse
to seek. It pins
my dreams onto shy
statues, and turns
time to jelly.
Setbacks slow cradled
are woken madly
once I'm defeated
in Monopoly.
Chances wrapped in 'Pass
The Parcel' paper
reveal my fate
and comic despair.
Life cons me then runs
away with the sunlight.
A patchwork doll remains.
It's a bugger, life.

Chisel '2013' Live

Chisel
doesn't fit the lock.
Why won't you turn for me?
Is it because
I have forgot
a chisel's not a key?

Chisel '2013' (Paper Edit)

Chisel.
Fit!
Turn!
Because
I forgot
a key.

Aliens Think I'm Their Leader

Minding my own business
and causing noone harm.
I noticed a strange creature
holding my left arm.

I knew it was an alien –
(Its name was on its head.)
I didn't want it near me.
(I thought I'd end up dead.)

I tried to run away from it,
but it clung to my arm,
and shouted 'You're our leader.
It's written in your palm.

Soon a million more of them
requested autograph,
but I told them I'm not Beckham,
so they shouldn't be so daft.

But I was who they followed.
They came especially,
to take a picture with me in
for their posterity.

I trembled as I mingled
with those from outer space,
who wanted me to wear a mask
to cover up my face.

Not wanting trouble, I agreed,
and did just what they said.
They gargled with excitement
then DJed on my head.

I hated being leader,
and said 'I'm not your man.
(although I do appreciate
you being such a fan.)

'As if you'd be our leader.'
They mockingly declared.
'We only came to say it
because we had been dared!'

Banned

Banned from Gamblers Anonymous
for being too well known,
and too damned lucky;
You matched 6 numbers
47 times,
Winning approximately
207.27 million pounds.

Missing

I missed you more than Nookie Bear,
Radio Rentals, Tupperware.

I missed you more than Duty Free,
Spectrum Graphics, You & Me.

I missed you more than Pat & Mick,
Right Said Fred and TV Quick.

I missed you more than Howard's Way,
'Re-record not fade away, Re-record not fade away'.

I missed you more than Agadoo,
Alec Gilroy, Betty Boo.

I missed you more than Chukie Egg,
Daley Thompson, Dr Legg.

You missed me more than twice when you tried to run me over!

I Tried To Buy You Flowers

I tried to buy you lilies
but I couldn't see it through,
so I ran off to Ann Summers
for a naughty toy or two.

I tried to buy you orchids
but I felt a little shy,
so I left to buy some vaseline,
and products from KY.

I tried to buy you daisies
but I came out in a rash,
so I ran off to the sex shop
for a little 'Porno' stash.

I tried to buy you roses
but I blushed and went bright red,
so I rushed off to the chemist
for some Durex packs instead.

I tried to buy you flowers,
but I never had much luck.
At least I've got the other things
If we want to have a . . . flipping good night in!

I Compare Thee To A Roast Dinner

As cool as a sprout,
and more fragrant than a cabbage –
you turned me on with your Yorkshire Pudding wit.

Your potato looks, and carrot personality
attracted me like gravy to a plate.
Your cauliflower skin and garden pea humour
was as passionate as a roast beef kiss.

Your solicitor was not impressed with this response to your
divorce proceedings.

Time

Time mocks us through its inconvenient ways.
It travels prestissimo, when souls soar;
slowing, like a full stop, when life's a chore.
It ridicules our inefficient days,
then when claiming to be faithful, it strays.
Affecting memories blanked out over
                    Time.

Like photographing oxygen; don't raise
hopes of capturing, and using for your
pleasure. We can't control the length it stays
as a companion on our lifelong tour,
yet in arrogance waste it, always sure
there's years to go before our landlord calls out
                    Time.

Fabricated Absurd Comic Truth

General

- It's a sign of good luck if the World ends on a Monday.
- There are only 27 cash points in the whole of London.
- In 1985 triangles nearly received an MBE for services to pool and snooker.
- In the 'Good Old Days' the alphabet was ordered differently. F came before U, and C was still after B.
- Jam is 20 today!
- An anagram of paint is panty.
- If you ask anyone to quote 3 random numbers between 7 and 94 their answers will always be 12, 8, 76 (in that order).
- Eating Double-Glazing is never recommended.
- The moon was invented by a soft drink company.
- House prices in the South are so high that nobody has moved since 1982.
- Dying in some cases is not healthy.
- 99% of House Parties do not stipulate that guests must dress like Hugh Laurie.
- Did you know that the internet has haemorrhoids?
- Pub Quizzes are so called because the first quizzes were solely based on pubs.
- Lollipops hate publicity.

- DVD killed the Video Star.

- Infamous heckler David Cameroon once yelled the world would be a better place if trees strangled bad people and took their place.

- DVDs of magpies and zebras do not sell too well because they are only in black and white.

- An anagram of H&M is M&S.

- Trains deliberately piss you off to make EastEnders more bearable.

- It is illegal . . .

- It is acceptable to build an emergency ice rink in Aylesbury if the temperature exceeds 32 degrees celsius.

- People who wear green a lot generally like the colour green.

- Andrew 'Shirley Bassey' Haddaway from Swansea is the 72nd most successful caravan breeder in the world.

- The moo-oink pact in 1927 was the first instance of animals allowing each other to make their farmyard sound. The Baaa-Quack pact in 2014 was the second.

- The London Eye visits an optician twice a year to ensure it hasn't got cataracts.

- What came first? The sandwich or toast? Toast. Fact!

- This week's winning bingo numbers are 7, 24, 34, -1, 72, 7, C#.

- It is highly unlikely that you would be able to buy pie charts and chips at a Launderette.

- In the 'old days' 60 pence could buy you Switzerland.

- The 2007 Social Networking Act made it illegal for any individual to claim someone as a friend unless they were added on Facebook.

- Self Assessment forms sometimes get sent to taxi firms by mistake.

- Smart Cars are members of MENSA.

- You are more likely to get a paperjam in your printer if there is also a jam on the corresponding motorway to your paper size. For example, if the A5 is congested and you are using A5 paper, you are more likely to get a paper jam.

- You should never allow a lion into your home unless it has got a valid search warrant.

-   | Custard Creams | vs | Digestives |
    | --- | --- | --- |
    | HobNobs | vs | Crunch Creams |
    | Chocolate Digestives | vs | Rich Tea |
    | Bourbons | vs | Gingernuts |

    These ties will take place in the week commencing January 15th.

    Chocolate Digestives 4/9F.

- Paper Jams are not bestsellers at Waitrose.

- The letter 'L' in the phonetic alphabet was originally going to be called 'Loughborough'

- There are 52 cars in a deck of cars.

Music

- If the Beatles hadn't invented music then Westlife would have.

- Noddy Holder was once part of Sade.

- The cello is the only stringed instrument to be in the union for wind instruments.

- Recorders secretly wish they were flutes.

- Lily Allen was originally going to be called Rhododendron Allen.

- Paulo Nutini is allergic to himself.
- In the Jungle the mighty jungle monkfish sleep tonight.
- Lady Ga Ga is also a skilled Java programmer.
- If you sing the scales backwards while playing the ukulele in your underpants you will need to have a very good reason.
- Blur were originally called Smudge.

Sport

- Speedway is illegal between 7.30am and 7.45am in the Pacific Ocean.
- Before the pole vault became so popular, dominoes was the number 1 pub sport in the world.
- Running the 100 metres in less than 12 seconds is impossible. Fact!
- Sponsoring a friend to run a marathon automatically means they are unable to win it.
- No 27 . . . Manchester United . . . will play . . .
- In 1967 Athletic events incorporated the now defunct shot jump. A competitor had to jump over a pole while a rival threw a shot at them. Points were awarded for height jumped, speed, and technical merit. There were only 956 fatalities.
- No 7 . . . Dale Winton
- The quarter final draw for the F.A Cup is the most watched programme in Liechtenstein.
- In a poll of young people under the age of 11, only one had ever heard of the darts player Leighton Rees.
- David Beckham had to be hypnotised in the dressing-room

before a game to ensure he did not take the goal kicks as well as corner kicks, free-kicks and penalty kicks.

- Sir Alex Ferguson sometimes got upset in his time management course if he thought it finished 3 minutes earlier than it should do.

- Up until 1971 there were 7 colours on traffic lights in the order of red, yellow, green, brown, blue, pink, black. This got reduced to three after the World Snooker Organisation paid half a leg of chalk for the other four and struck an agreement with the World Traffic Light Foundation for rights to the other 3.

- Tug-of-war never gets shown on TV because the BBC and ITV keep debating who should show it.

- Steve Davis eats and sleeps on snooker tables.

- Freddie Flintoff is so powerful that Old Trafford once moved 3 feet to the right after a spell of his bowling.

- Sebastian Vettel decided to become a motor racing driver after he drove his milk float so fast that all the eggs smashed.

Politics

- In the 1950s MPs considered a word tax for those who talked too much. After debating it for 27 years they decided to scrap the idea.

- MPs who win at bingo sometimes claim for a second House.

- Before any perspective MP is selected by their party they have to take a truth test. Anyone who scores less than 20% is automatically selected by their party.

- Politics never existed before Sir Winston Churchill.

- Andrew Marr loves politics so much that he had his house re-designed to resemble the House of Commons.
- There has never been a female prime minister
- The Conservative Party comes from the Latin 'Conservatory Partyie'.
- Nick Clegg and David Cameron send each other love notes at PMQs
- Oliver Cromwell banned Christmas because he was fearful of another Cliff Richard seasonal release.
- All the MPs have to conga out of the House of Commons after PMQs finish.

Science

- Before gravity was invented the sea and the sky were the other way around.
- Half a million silly people wear face masks when using their PCs in case they catch a computer virus.
- Coal is still used as currency in some mining communities.
- The sun was once green until the great custard experiment in 1432 went horrifically wrong and scarred the sun for life.
- Children are so stupid that they do not know how to split an atom.
- Google is the Roman god of beetroot.
- The World Health Organisation say that the 'Mind the Gap' pandemic at Clapham Junction is unstoppable.
- Dr Stephen Hawking eats his meals off the periodic table.
- The periodic table needs to have one of its legs replacing in the year 2037.

TV

- Deal or Canterbury? Canterbury.

- TV channels only know what they are broadcasting for the week when they read it in the papers.

- An elephant can hold its breath under water for an entire episode of Doc Martin.

- Rioting has only occurred once on Deal Or No Deal. It was when the contestant didn't use numerology to decide which boxes to select.

- Chris Tarrant laughs hysterically when he asks for a drink and the barman says 'But I don't want to give you that'

- Carry On On The Buses was voted the best comedy film never made.

- Newton & Ridley, the brewery in Coronation Street, is named after Sir Isaac Newton and Ridley Scott.

- The funniest TV shows are rarely made because TV execs die laughing from the concept.

- A focus group is recommending that Jeremy Vine dresses up as Batman because Panorama is so depressing.

- Come Dine With Me is on so often due an administration error. Only 20 episodes were officially commissioned, not the 20,000 that was keyed into the database.

- The BBC had to clone Nick Knowles after they realised they needed him to record 4 TV shows at the same time.

Also from Desert Hearts:

Quaking in Me Stackheels

A Beginner's Guide to Surviving Your First Public Performance

Paul Eccentric

Have you got what it takes to stand up on a stage in front of a sea of expectant strangers and wow them with your pearls of wit and wisdom or are you too scared of what might happen to you if the crowd suddenly turned ugly? Remember, there are more of them than there are of you and they know who you are! Have you ever wanted to know how to control an audience or to put a heckler in their place? Would you know how to prepare your show for maximum audience impact? And what exactly do you know about microphone technique and presentation? If you are a singer, a poet, a comedian or a public speaker of any kind; or if you would just like to know how to appear more confident in company than you naturally feel, then let Paul Eccentric, performance poet, singer, stage director, compere and all-round show-off, talk you through the tricks of the trade, learned the hard way over his 25-year career stomping the boards in big boots... Invaluable lessons for any would-be performer!

Paul Eccentric is a poet, novelist, singer, lyricist, playwright and director. He has also been coaching performers in the art of confidence and surviving their first night since 2009. Among his various musical forays into the worlds of jazz, punk, polka, skiffle, swing and doowop, Paul has both written and sung for The Odd Eccentric since 1984 and The Senti-Mentals since 1998. He has published two solo poetry collections Lyrical Quibble & Quip and The Kult of the Kazoo, and a novel Down Among the Ordinaries. As one half of The Antipoet he has released two beat poetry CDs, Tights Not Stockings and Hanging with Poets. His most recent albums Odds 'n Sods and Who Knows, Who Cares? are available from Doopop Records.